W9-BWG-433

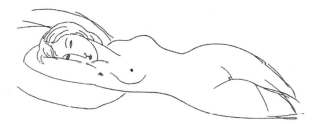

77 LOVE SONNETS

99 LOVE SONNETS

77 *Love Sonnets*

---

by Garrison Keillor

Published by
Common Good Books
165 Western Avenue North
St. Paul, Minnesota 55102
www.commongoodbooks.com

Copyright ©2009 by Garrison Keillor
All rights reserved
Distributed in the United States of America by Viking Penguin

Designed by Paul Buckley
Printed in the United States of America
Set in Eldorado Text

The Library of Congress has cataloged this edition as follows:
2009923492
Paperback ISBN-13: 978-0-14-311527-4

CONTENTS

1

2

3

4

5

6

7

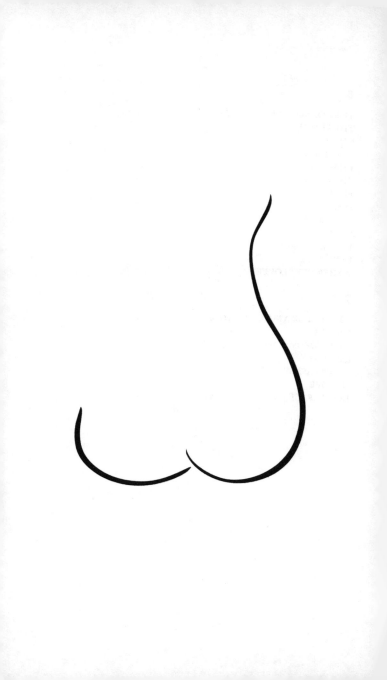

1

Here I am O Lord and here is my prayer:

Please be there.

Don't want to ask too much, miracles and such—

Just whisper in the air: please be there.

When I die like other folks,

Don't want to find out You're a hoax.

So I'm not on my knees asking for world peace

Or that the polar icecap freeze

And save the polar bear

Or even that the poor be fed

Or angels hover o'er my bed

But I will sure be pissed

If I should have been an atheist.

O Lord, please exist.

You made crusty bread rolls filled with chunks of brie
And minced garlic drizzled with olive oil
And baked them until the brie was bubbly
And we ate them lovingly, our legs coiled
Together under the table. And salmon with dill
And lemon and whole-wheat couscous
Baked with garlic and fresh ginger, and a hill
Of green beans and carrots roasted with honey and tofu.
It was beautiful, the candles, the linen and silver,
The sun shining down on our northern street,
Me with my hand on your leg. You, my lover,
In your jeans and green T-shirt and beautiful bare feet.
　　How simple life is. We buy a fish. We are fed.
　　We sit close to each other, we talk and then we go to bed.

You lay your head on my arm and soon your eyes
Close and your breathing is slow, your sweet
Lips part, where we lie on your bed crosswise,
The cars whispering past on the dark street.
You are so beautiful. The candle flickers on the shelf,
The clock ticks. The neighbors are gone to bed.
The city sleeps. I have you all to myself,
The loyal guardian of your lovely head.
I pray that ice will never touch your heart
And that you thrive and bloom like the apple tree.
And may you rise up valiant when we part,
And when you are old keep some fond thoughts of me.
    Goodnight my love, you of all the loveliest.
    The angels smile on you as you take your rest.

Once after dinner this woman and I walked past
An empty basketball court and she says,
"I played on a team my junior year in Belfast,"
And I said, "Want to shoot some?" She said, "Yes,"
Though she was wearing a long black dinner dress.
She kicked off her high heels and she caught
My pass and with great finesse
Drove to the baseline, jumped and shot.
Swish. Two points. We played for awhile,
Man in a black suit, woman in a long black gown.
I loved her quickness and her heads-up style,
Her cool hand as she beat me hands down—

    She is the shooting star of the Black Irish Squad
    And I am the man who sets her up, by God.

Shall I compare thee to a summer's day?
Shakespeare already did that, long before us
So I will compare thee to a summer's night, okay?
Vibrating keenly like this insect chorus.

We perched last night in our backyard
Under a full moon, drinking cold mint tea,
Old couples out for a stroll on the boulevard,
And a bat flew by and I touched your bare brown knee

And right then those words did not need to be said
About the goodness of the past twelve years,
Why I don't regret the tangle of events that led
Me through the bad patches to be sitting here

Now with you, under this particular Midwestern sky
On a perfect evening at the beginning of July.

A hard year and trouble brewing everywhere,
Insurance companies and banks sliding headfirst
Toward oblivion at 50 cents a share
And heading south. The bubble has burst
And our mortgaged castle in the air
Will likely crash and burn, but don't despair,
Though probably our pension fund is cursed.
For still we have this lovely love affair
In which we are so steadily immersed
And if we must go on welfare and wear
Used clothes and live on angel hair and liverwurst,
Still I'll smile whenever I see you there,
Bathing in the creek behind our shack.
I'll love you still and hope you love me back.

Dozy in August on a battered screened porch
Overlooking a green meadow as 24 Holstein cows
Swaying enormous white udders march
Down the dirt road to the barn behind the house.
We rock in the ancient chairs, languorously,
Listening to an old farmer reminisce
About those who sat here long before you and me
And drank black coffee as weak as this
And anguished over perilous sickness and war
And thought, as we do, about the basic mysteries.
They took some comfort from this porch
On just such placid afternoons as these.

    The bumblebees are blitzing the sunflowers.
    God owns tomorrow but today is ours.

Eternal light on you, Brother John, my hero,
A good worker, cheerful and ambitious,
Who sat daily at your desk to fill the narrow
Pages with a clear stream of delicious
Painterly thought and homage to the sweet
Particulars of earth. I shook your hand
On the train downtown from 155th Street,
You, grinning, white hair, blessed blessed man
Like a boy going away to school. "Goodbye,"
I said. "See you soon." You grinned.
I think you knew you were soon to die,
And away the train went with a whoosh of wind.
    You blessed me once, my older brother John.
    You left so suddenly. The family struggles on.

I grew up in a northern town
Ground was flat for miles around
Everyone was Calvinist
Underwear was in a twist
Angry and obsessed with sin
Sunlight almost did us in
I was young and very pure
Until I was sweet sixteen
And then I read great literature
That said the world is sweet and green—
So live your life and seize the day
Before the flowers fade away.
    And now I try to smell the roses
    Which are God's doing, one supposes.

I dreaded a life of domestic religion,
The pastel rambler, two-car garage, lawn mower,
The peevish voice of the wife in the kitchen,
And me with nothing wonderful to show her.
I wanted to live several lives, which meant
Abandoning some. I was unfaithful
To good women and left them for something different,
Something salty, mysterious. I was wasteful.
But now I have grown much too fond of this
Screened porch, the majestic terrace with a view
Of river valley, the kitchen, the deliciousness
Of coffee and music, to look for something new.
    Though sometimes I awaken at first light
    And feel the urge— get up, get going out of sight.

Up in the sky the lovers lay in bed
Naked, face to face and hip to thigh,
Her leg between his legs, his arm beneath her head,
Their hands roaming freely, up in the sky.
In the dark, Manhattan lay at their feet,
A blanket of glittering stars thrown down.
Beyond her bare shoulder, 59th Street,
And from her left ankle the buses headed uptown.
They came to the city for romance, as people do,
And with each other they scaled the heights,
And now, united, they lie at rest, these two,
The bed gently rocking in the sea of lights.

    Where will they go? What happens next? I do not know.
    I am that man waiting at the bus stop far below.

The tennis players volley on the bright green court,
Slipping and sliding to and fro while up above
Them, spread naked on a bed in room 704,
A young woman sings the aria of burning love—
Her lover's head between her legs, her feet on his back,
And she is singing for pleasure, while outside
The streets are cleaned, construction is on track,
The buses come on time and people board and ride
And she lies, eyes closed, hands holding his, and moans
As he addresses her with all deliberate passion.
And the clerks sort the mail into the correct zones
And all the ATM machines have sufficient cash in.
 Good sir, don't stop. We each must do our duty.
 Some drive the bus and others drive the beauty.

How beautiful and simple here
the woman looking at the mirror
through a little camera lens
at her own magnificence
finger of her left hand curled
on the shutter a naked girl
tall and tan in perfect health
looking calmly at herself
squinting one blue green eye
taking a photograph that I
regard with reverence and love
to her a simple matter of
clicking the shutter to preserve
on film her beauty and her nerve

On a winter afternoon she plays Chopin,
A wistful piano étude on a snowy day,
Skidding on a tricky passage in the left hand,
Trying to tell me in a delicate way
That even in this cold season love can endure
And be green again, which I do want to believe,
Despite my unconstant heart— I crave more
Love, more and more and still more— to give
Affection by the bushel! I don't want to schedule
Love, I want it to pour out— a round of songs,
Feasts, the delirium of dance, total capitul-
Ation, a flight to Paris— and then it bongs,

>The old clock in the corner. Ten times. It's dark,
>And I'm old, and O how beautiful you are.

When my body and your body
Lie together under a white sheet
Your head on my arm
Your leg thrown over my leg
The whole long continent of you
The pale ridgeline of your ribcage and hip and thigh
Neighbor to me
There is nothing that needs to be explained
Or accomplished, the world is at rest and complete
And though
We drift apart in the eddies of the day
We will find our way back
To the slight hollows that mark the place
Where we lie now, astonished, saying nothing.

Is it cold enough for you? the neighbor inquires,
Shoveling this gray world that only gets grayer,
Dirty snow and the haze from our home fires
Rising in the sky like impossible prayers:
God give me a good heart for Lent,
God spare me my just punishment.
Fingers of snow across the gray sidewalk,
Shovels scraping up and down the block.
St. Paul, Minnesota, is where I'm at.
Above is a gray aluminum sky,
Below is the grave where I must lie.
Beyond is the prairie frozen hard and flat.
> How did I come to this city of disappointed men?
> O that my young love were in my arms again.

Driving the 101 doing eighty-five at quarter to three

In the morning, white reflectors flashing the lanes,

You with your head on my shoulder asleep,

I wish we'd cross over the Sierra range

And keep driving, darling, on and on

To Las Vegas, tomorrow the Grand Canyon,

Make the Mexican border Thursday at dawn,

Head for the tropics and abandon

The sandstone solemnity of St. Paul

For a beach house, the waves galumping on the shore,

Birds skittering, salt air— darling I want to fall

Out of my pensive life and be lost in yours.

    But we stop in the city. Baffled. And then

    In the morning resume our secret lives again.

A COUPLE ON THE STREET

Apparently they are a scandalous pair,
Strolling the main drag, not quite hand in hand,
The tall young woman and the dazed old man.
And old ladies turn like wounded birds and stare
And shake their great red wattles and curse
And young women smirk at this ludicrous romance—
But see how tenderly his eyes seek hers
And their elbows brush— and, defiant, they hold hands
And dare to gaze at each other. She is avid
To be loved and love leaps up from them
As music sprang from Mozart, and they can have it
All, *Don Giovanni* and then the *Requiem*.

"Fools!" the ladies cry. "It should not and it cannot be!"
And they are right. But O the sweetness and the courtesy.

Let them talk about us if they like. I don't care.
I am engrossed in your excellent profile,
Your noble nose and quick lips and mahogany hair
Clipped up high in a Grecian goddess pile.
You are of all women the most exquisite,
Most elegant in or out of clothes,
And I remove them and my own and we visit
In your great flowery bed and my heart goes
Galump-galump— and when you say,
"Put your fingers here, curved just so
And bite me gently there— I'll turn this way—
Yes, like that— "and on and on we go
Up to the top and Boom and then the slow descent,
Me spooned behind you, curved and quietly content.

Here by the enormous swimming pool at the Biltmore
Twenty-six young dark-skinned women lie
In tiny bikinis like mermaids on the shore,
And I, bound for Ithaca, just sail on by,
Heading for you, Penelope, to tell the tale,
How that whole Trojan War gave me the willies,
The pointlessness of it, and I set sail,
Having paid off Homer and left Achilles
In his tent, and was lucky to get a favorable wind
And stopped here at the Biltmore to recompute
My course, and found twenty-six dark-skinned
Women, their breasts displayed like fresh fruit.

    Thanks but no thanks. They only want a tan.
    You, dear, love a good story. I'm your man.

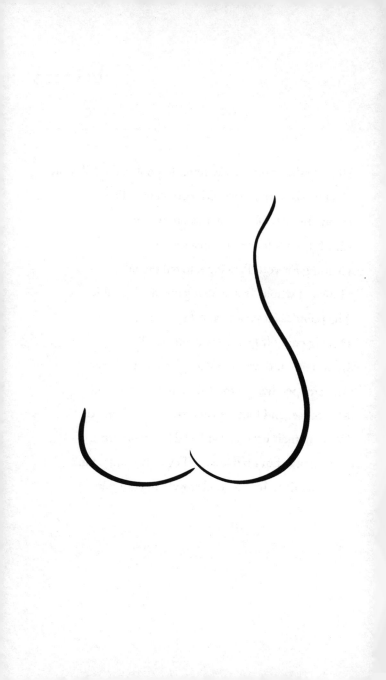

I'm a radio man for thirty-five years
Doing an old variety show
Based on some I used to hear
When I was your age long ago.
Critics pointed out my debts
To Bob & Ray and Fibber McGee
But alcohol and cigarettes
Swept those critics out to sea
And to twenty-year-olds who were born
Too late to hear the great Fred Allen,
I'm the inventor of the form,
Sailing the airwaves like Magellan.
    A thief who escapes and is not hung
    May yet be honored by the young.

Bryn Mawr girl in the plaid skirt and sweater set
Working at The New Yorker in the summer of '69,
Reading unsolicited stories through the cigarette
Smoke, thank you, dear, for rescuing mine.

You sent it upstairs with your blessing, a green slip,
Telling the editor to read it, and he read it,
And your gift of attention launched my little ship
Off in the direction it still is headed.

Years have passed since you smiled at me and saved
Me from a life of failure, my sweet.
And I bless you for the gift you gave,
My unknown angel of 25 West 43rd Street.

I have done some good work. Lord knows I've tried,
And yet the importance of angels cannot be denied.

The secret of a long career is simply to not fade
Or think about your reputation for one minute.
It's like becoming Tallest Boy In The Sixth Grade,
Stick around and you're bound to win it.
Fyodor Dostoevsky took his own sweet time
And found a punishment to fit the crime,
And slowly as a centipede trots off
He wrote *The Brothers Karamazov*.
After years Mrs. Joyce cried out in bliss, "He's
Finally finished with *Ulysses*."
James had a smoke and took a break,
Then started in on *Finnegans Wake*.

    So do your work, keep going straight ahead,
    And you can be a genius someday after you are dead.

She's a show girl, my girl, hands on hips,
Best foot forward and a million-dollar smile—
"I've got sunshine" and she spins, shimmies, dips—
Hey! It's America's No. 1 ten-year-old child.
Math, reading, yes, yes, and swimming— a good strong
Butterfly— but she lights up at "My Guy."
When we hold hands, we sing the Beatles song,
And in the car, it's a grand old flag flying high.
It's good to be ten. You love your parents
And tearing around and the flag is grand
And you swim against the powerful currents
Of heredity and yet you want to hold my hand.
   You're a high-flying girl, and the water is wide,
   And when you touch me, I feel happy inside.

She is ten. "I love you. So much," she tells me
On the phone in the evening. She loves this phrase
And "I miss you. So much." I'm in Knoxville, Tennessee,
En route to Phoenix, on the road for six days.
Four to go. Airports, freeways, Holiday Inns,
Denny's, *USA Today*, highway America.
Every night, audiences expecting the genuine,
And me, lonely, on the road through Jericho.
It's an okay life. Dangerous but okay.
I don't drink, don't stay out late. I eat right.
But the lonesome road blues follows me around all day
And there are rocks and nails in my bed at night.

    I think about her. I miss her. I get dressed
    And go tell stories about families in the Midwest.

I went dancing one night in East Lansing
And Minot was hot as could be
I found what my heart wants in Oshkosh, Wisconsin,
And in Omaha saw a home what's for me.
We had a thrilling sojourn in Billings
And necked in the dark in Bismarck
And were even more torrid in Fargo-Moorhead
And dances in Kansas lit romance's spark.
We sowed wild grains across the Great Plains,
Flung out our youth in Duluth,
Found euphoria and joy in Peoria, Illinois,
Had a ball in St. Paul— it's the absolute truth.
    Why should we fly off to Paris or Rome?
    We have long summer nights right here at home.

COLUMBUS, GEORGIA

Sweet town where the seductive magnolia grows,

Home of barbecue with mustardy sauce on it,

Down where the old Chattahoochee flows.

Doggone, you make me feel like whomping up a sonnet!

Let me not to the marriage of pork and sauce

Admit impediments. Nosirree.

Fix me up a plate of it, hoss.

And I'll sit and eat it slow. I'm in no hurry.

And then I will sing you a slow blues

About Ma Rainey and Carson McCullers who were from

here,

And I sing, "Anything you want bad you are bound to lose

So you may as well set down and enjoy a cold beer."

Life is a bitch but y'all can affordja

A real nice summer afternoon in Columbus, Georgia.

Let me sing of the great buffet that is Baltimore
And of crabs boiled, fried, or sautéed,
Brought in by boat from the Eastern Shore
And eaten in small cafes along the Bay,
On Charles Street, Fells Point, or Pimlico.
In a neighborhood joint called Al's or Mel's,
Good eaters sit at the counter in a row
Like old heavyweights awaiting the bell.
Sit with enormous napkins on their laps
And order up the Seafood Combination—
Oysters, scallops, lobster, crabs, more crabs,
A sensational crustacean celebration.

    Tuck in your napkin, put your feet on the floor.
    Let's eat. It's time. We're in Baltimore.

My plane landed, I'm in a cab (only carry-on,
No waiting) and racing from LaGuardia to you.
Just time to write a sonnet. My driver Tran
Van Vo, has a QuikPass and we shoot through
The tollgate on the Triborough and head
Down the FDR to 96th and then west
And I could call you on the cell but instead
Imagine you, pacing the floor, dressed
In shorts and T-shirt, listening to *Morning Edition.*
I'll ditch this dark suit and we will resume
Our stately life and the excellent tradition
Of sex after breakfast. The dark bedroom
    Awaits. But now the traffic slows— O God, the torture,
    Adam held up in traffic, Eve pacing the orchard.

The first time we met was in Docks Cafe.
We talked for hours though I didn't know what to say.
The second was at Café des Artistes with those murals
Of Edwardian gentlemen and semi-naked girls.
And that night we stood on a 12th floor terrace
Overlooking roofs and chimneys like in Paris
Except in New York. I asked if I could kiss you
Which turned out not to be an issue.
You were thirty-five and enjoyed being pursued
And two weeks later, in an extravagant mood,
Our romance took a sharp turn north,
And afterward, listening to Mahler's Fourth,
> We lay entwined in a bed near the Boston Common.
> Thank you, Lord, for fifteen years since then. Amen.

Frankie and Johnny were lovers and swore to be true

To each other and it didn't take him all that long

Before he went to the hotel with You Know Who

And got busy doing Miss Frankie wrong.

He was her man, a good lover, handsome

In his bowler and spats, but not so astute,

Which led to her looking over the hotel transom

And pulling out the .44 which went rooty-toot-toot.

And the rubber-tired hearses came and poor Frankie

Was locked up in a dungeon cell. They threw

Away the key. She lay and wept in her hanky

But mostly she felt like a fool. Wouldn't you?

    People had warned her, again and again and again.

    And she knew it too. There is no good in men.

THE ANGER OF WOMEN

The anger of women pervades the rooms
Like a cold snap, and you wait for the thaw
To open the window and air out the anger fumes,
And then a right hook KA-POW to the jaw!
And she says three jagged things about you
And then it's over. She bursts into tears,
The storm spent, the sky turns sky-blue.
But a man's heart can hurt for many years.
I have found the anger of women unbearable.
And when my goddesses have cursed the day
They met me and said those terrible
Things, I folded my tent and stole away.
    I yielded to their righteous dominion
    And went off in search of another opinion.

Not all dark thoughts need be expressed—
The early death you've always feared,
Your heart fluttering in your chest,
The feeling that your outfit's weird,
You're getting fat, the plane might fall
Screaming out of the sky and plow
Into the mountain and we all
Die— let's not discuss it now.
Let's talk about last night at the Met
When we saw *Der Rosenkavalier*,
That glorious Act III waltz duet
We loved from seats far to the rear.

    Not all dark thoughts need be expressed.
    Know that I love you. Ignore the rest.

Out of the flat dry country where I seem to be
Stuck these days I'd like to cruise down the Nile
On a ship with reference librarians and you and me
In white linen outfits, Italian style.
We'd sashay down to supper in the grand salon,
Champagne and oysters, and under Egyptian stars,
We'd dance a two-step topside until dawn
As the ancient black piano-player in the bar
Plays "Love Walked In" and "If I Had You"
Which, in my case, I do, and then at the bow
We'd look forward to the beautiful faint blue
Glimmer of somewhere we'll get to somehow.

     We are stowaways enjoying free room and board.
     And each day, my darling, is its own reward.

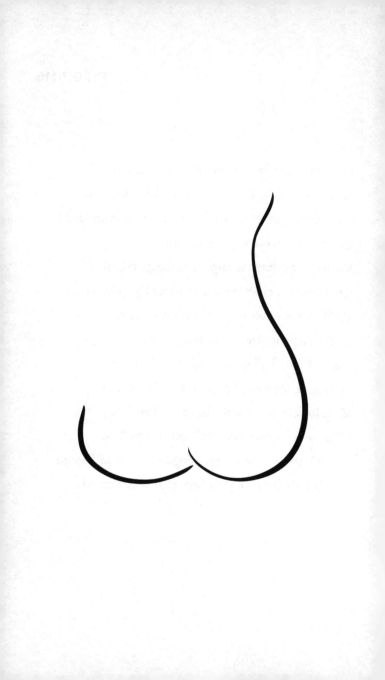

3

ON THE OPENING OF A NEW BOOKSTORE

On the high hill above the river in St. Paul,
Against the advice of civil engineers,
The Archbishop insisted his Cathedral stand tall
And stone gray, and so it has for eighty years.
Back behind its magnificence, on drowsy streets
Of gabled houses, brick and stone and wood,
Are a thousand stories of the daily feats
Of courage that are love and parenthood.
Each lighted window represents an enterprise
By strangers whom I feel I ought to know
And so, in a bookstore with windows to the skies,
I sit and read heroic tales of long ago.

A cold fall day and we are strangers, far apart.
But in these books I find some secrets of your heart.

THE LOST SON

There is so very little we can do,
Friends, for these beautiful children of ours,
They will come to grief and suffer and you
And I bow to darkness and evil powers.

The gentle boy who wrote poems goes
For a walk in January and does not return.
His mother and father search the woods. The snow
Is deep. All night their hearts burn

For him. He is found, hanging from a limb,
And the father carries the body of his son
Into the yard and tenderly lays him
On the step. Stephen, O darling one,

See how your parents' hearts break for you.
There is so very little we can do.

SONNET FOR MARY

The old lady marching along Concourse A
Rather slowly in front of you is making her way
To get on a plane to fly out to Denver.
Though she is in pain, she would not complain ever.
She walks all bent over. She's 81.
But her sister died and there's work to be done.
She must bury her sister and clean out the condo
And see to her niece who's retarded, sweet Rhonda.
There's a funeral to arrange, a condo to sell,
And a 50-year-old child who can't care for herself.
How will she do it so far from home?
God will provide Who looks after His own.
    And so I recite a short prayer every day
    For all the old ladies who are making their way.

MIAMI SONNET

A parade of couples tonight one after another
Two by two toward the open-air cafes
On the pier for Friday night supper.
No talk, no mutual glances, their faces dazed
With boredom, they walk under the shining
Marquees of Cuban, Italian, the romantic cuisines,
And enter their steel stanchions for dining,
Like prisoners heading for the guillotine.
All my life I fled from that. I still flee
From dumb boredom. I endure dramatic revisions,
Sudden departures, divorce, and now I see
The fugitive is imprisoned by the fear of prison.
    I sit alone with rice and beans and a ginger beer,
    No one to tell this to but you and you're not here.

We marry in sunshine on a field of green
And vow to last forever and old ladies cry
And wish us well and soon come those small mean
Arguments about what was said. You and I
Sit, not looking at each other this morning,
Listening to the waves of the radio,
And breakfast is cold burnt toast, a warning
That this house will fall in a year or so.
Oh darling, I make this last stupid appeal—
Look at me. Speak to me. Let's not be caught
In a duel of silences. Let's say what we feel—
That I love you, and you love me, or not, if not.

    And if not, I will go away. That's not a threat.
    But I refuse to die for love, my darling. Not yet.

A summer night and the moon, the far cry of a semi,
The Milky Way, crickets chittering in the flowers.
I seem to be boring you, my darling, am I?
We haven't said much for the past two hours.
I love you but maybe it would be intrusive
To say so and you'd feel conflicted— I mean,
Maybe there's an old lover you got news of
Who's back in town from far away. Eugene.
You can never forget the night you and he kissed,
Your mouths sweet with Sauvignon Blanc—
What a guy! and here I am, an old journalist
Who uses Listerine and talks too loud, honk honk.
    I'm going to bed. I have to be at work by nine.
    Goodnight. See you tomorrow. Why are you crying?

A lacerating lecture late at night. I hear
All my sins laid out with great force
Of conviction and every sentence is sincere
And well-deserved. Someone standing outdoors
On the terrace would see a woman in anguish,
A solemn man in a chair. She is pacing,
Gesturing, and he sits like a distinguished
Senator convicted of mail fraud and facing
Prison. I'm sorry. It was all wrong.
The courtship, the happiness, the wedding day,
The house and yard— darling, I don't belong
In marriage. I plead guilty. Send me away

    To Leavenworth out on the Kansas prairie.
    And let them put me into solitary.

Life is absurd. A man can count on that.
After the great triumph, you're left standing alone,
Standing on the corner, holding your hat,
Trying to call a friend on your cell phone.
Men my age are arrested for public exposure
Who only needed to take a leak in the bushes.
They didn't run through the park with no clothes or
Flash anyone. Life is like that. Some parts precious,
Moments of glory, and then the need for urination,
Then a disgrace in men's eyes, and crying bootlessly.
Here I am, a man of a certain reputation,
But your love, darling, is worth all of that to me.

    Were I an outlaw, branded far and wide, No Good,
    You'd love me just the same. I know you would.

BLACK SHIRT

You and I first made love on a January night
And two years later I remember that room
Where we sat, the fireplace, the bed, and which light
Was on by the bed and what was said by whom,
Your jeans on the floor and your black shirt,
You leading me to be your lover
And how I forgot everything else on earth
For those hours and we seemed to hover
Timeless in the confines of each other.
And ever since, even on the rockiest day,
I recall your eyes, your voice, the shudder
Of pleasure and how peacefully we lay,
    And you said, "Either I go now or stay the night,"
    And didn't move, and then the morning light.

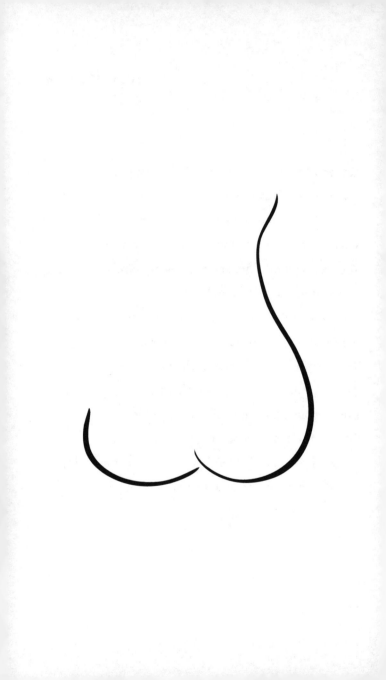

4

Two-thousand nine, the 20th of January,
At the Capitol I stood out in the freezing cold
With two million kinsmen, feeling very
Warm and bountiful as the big drums rolled
And the man said the oath, so help me God,
And cannons boomed and all of us— O we cried,
We cried, old black ladies and me, and applauded.
We wept, America, for you justified
At last as a nation of by God true ideals,
True beginnings, to which we now return—
Created equal, justice under law— one feels
That even in the cold, these fires burn.
> And then the man and his wife walking down the street
> And the country moves to a redemption beat.

SONNET FOR JULIE'S BIRTHDAY

My eyes get misty when I think of Julie Christie—
If a man wished to be kissed he
Would want it to be her lips.
Darling Julie, I love you truly,
You'd make a king a fool— he
Would launch a thousand ships.
And today you are turning 66!
Time is still playing its cruel little tricks.
I see you walking through the snow
Looking for your lover Dr. Zhivago
In the bad old days of long ago
As the czar and czarina and the bourgeois go
Off to a grim fate in the gulag archipelago.
Let's go to the Four Seasons in Chicago.

He fought in the Pacific campaign, flying a B-24,
A kid in a flight jacket, in the clean blue cold.
He mostly didn't say much about the war
But down deep he stayed 23 years old
And looked at the big brass with a narrow eye
And when they said, Line up here, he went over there.
A long life and right up until he waved goodbye
He was improvising, flying on a wing and a prayer.
Skirting the clouds, daring, working by feel,
Poking his camera through the door, lifting the lid,
Willing to be lucky: that was his deal,
And in his memory, we could do the same, kid.

    To give up authority and simply try to see.
    I'll look out for you, kid, you watch out for me.

George Bizet was born in Omaha. He was Lutheran bred,
His real name was Duane. He was in 4H.
He earned a blue ribbon for building a shed
But felt "different" from a very young age.
He walked around town in a black beret.
 Something French in him needed to be expressed,
He felt, and one fine *printemps* day in May
He told his mother, "Maman, I'm leaving the Midwest."
She cried, "It would break our hearts if you leave!"
He said, "Maman, I am not cut out for farmin'!
My *je ne sais quoi* is *joie de vivre*"—
And that night he said to his girlfriend Carmen,

> "Darling, it's cold here and the water tastes like copper. A
> Plane leaves for Paris at midnight. Let's be an opera."

CHRISTINE

Christine was the smartest girl in the eleventh grade,
Tall with dark hair tied up in a tight French braid,
The only girl I knew who read Albert Camus,
And for that very reason I did, too.

I stood behind her in choir, a lonesome baritone,
But when I smelled her exotic French cologne
And felt the existential heat of her body,
I became Luciano Pavarotti.

In chorus when I was seventeen
I met the mysterious Christine,
The tall dark girl whom I adored
And when we sang praises to the Lord
I gave praise to the back of Christine's head
And sang to her what never could be said.

"Function follows form," said Louis Sullivan one warm
Evening in Chicago over beer. His wife said, "Dear,
I think you meant it the other way around."
Sullivan looked at her and frowned.
"Okay, form follows function," he said.
A light bulb flickered over his head,
A spark of architectural brilliance
That soon would dazzle millions.
"Write it down," she said. "Here's a pencil."
And soon he was enormously influential
And thanks to his wife's correction,
Architecture headed in a functional direction.

    But he often wondered if maybe he had been mistook
    And if things should be used according to how they
look.

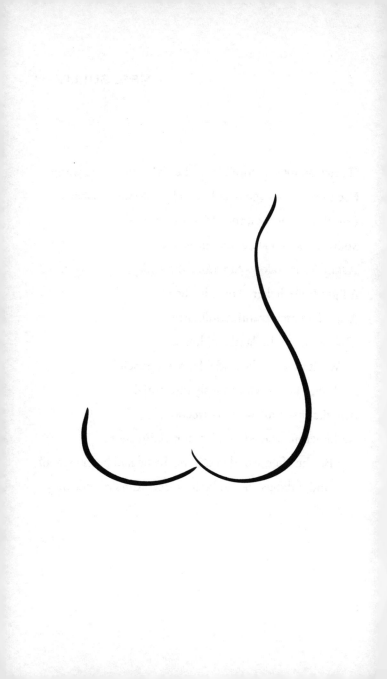

5

Another year gone and the old man with the scythe
Is mowing closer. He hasn't been subtle, has he.
Too many good people gone, and I could sit and cry
For them— except that you look exceptionally snazzy
And sexy despite the miles on your odometer,
As if you have a few more aces up your sleeve.
Maybe you were born under a lucky comet or
Maybe it's just the delirium of New Year's Eve.
I gaze in your face and take your hand— you're
Positively glowing. Maybe we've been sorry a
Long enough time and now we get some grandeur
And do our dance and sing our aria.

    May the New Year bring us before it has flown
    All we would have wished for had we only known.

It is a strange winter, January mixed in with April,
A cold snap and the next day everything thaws,
And you wonder if the buses run and if the morning paper'll
Come this morning— if we can still trust in natural laws.

We worry about our grandchildren and greenhouse gases
And then we get in the car and venture forth
In blind faith that a bad spell eventually passes,
A faith we were brought up with here in the North.

We are taciturn people and we have known dark nights
When ghosts attacked us and recrimination and remorse,
And we got up, put on a bathrobe, turned on a few lights,
Made tea, and said nothing about it to anyone of course.

And when spring comes, and the crocuses and purple gentian,
I'd like to undress you, though it's nothing I would ever
mention.

It's March in St. Paul. Eight a.m. A pale
Frozen mist in the air. The snow is gritty gray
Around the stone statue of Nathan Hale.
Scott Fitzgerald walks here almost every day
Hand in hand with Bessie Smith, or Maria Callas,
And Franz Kafka and Judy Garland stroll in the snow
And Princess Diana escapes from Kensington Palace
To meet Jack Kennedy and Marilyn Monroe.
They all look calm and very elegant indeed,
Despite all the grief they've been through.
To comprehend a nectar requires sorest need,
So said Emily Dickinson. (She's here, too.)

    Life is tragic. Oh God, the miseries we bear
    But it's always good to get out in the fresh air.

March and Lent and we march along on our spiritual journeys
As winter hangs on and the world looks older and duller
And then in the mail comes the spring seed catalogue
from Gurney's
And suddenly there is life and audacious color
And excitement rivaling Times Square or Las Vegas—
Blue Lake, Early Fortune, King of the Garden beans,
Stunning onions, phenomenal fennel, and big brutes of
rutabagas,
And the beet that can't be beat: the extra-early Ruby Queens.
And O the tomatoes! Bearers of pure joy!
From tasteless store-bought stuff, deliver us!
The Crimson Defender, and Pink Delight, and Big Boy,
And the Beef Eater—the tomato carnivorous.
      Lord, whose Arm is powerful, whose Word is valid,
      Preserve us until July when we'll have salad.

We're here to honor those who went to war
And did not mean to die, but did die, grievously,
In eighteen sixty-one and in two-thousand four
Though they were amiable as you or me.
Young and hopeful, knowing little of horror—
Singers and athletes, and gently bred.
Good sergeants turned them into warriors,
And at the end, they were moving straight ahead.
As we look at these gravestones, row on row on row,
See the men as they were, laughing and joking,
On that bright irreverent morning long ago,
And once more, let our hearts be broken.

God have mercy on them for their unhappy gift.
May we live the good lives they might have lived.

Be free, dear graduate. That's what my advice is:
And if it's trouble for which you hunger,
Don't wait for midlife to have your crisis.
It's better to do it when you're younger.
Don't wait until you're older and at the pinnacle
And people fawn over you and hail your
So-called achievements. Not to be cynical,
But youth is the best time for a big bold failure.
You won't learn this from reading Plato or Socrates:
But rather than average, why not go for Really Really Bad?
Better to be a fool than one of the mediocrities.
And a major failure can bring you closer to your dad.

> Fritter away your dough. Don't plan, don't build.
> He's waiting. That fatted calf needs to be killed.

O summer here you are sh-bop sh-bop yeah yeah whoa whoa
And we are driving around town tonight hey hey hey
The windows wide open and the Beach Boys on the radio
And we'll have fun fun fun til Daddy takes the T-bird away
Which Daddy will do and then we must Make Some-
thing of our lives
And climb the steep slope like good little Sherpas
And become daddies ourselves and our good wives
Will frown if we drive anywhere without a clear purpose
But tonight I am cruising for no reason around St. Paul
And I remember those innocent girls I used to hang
Around with when we had no place to go at all
Except around and around, the radio playing shang
shang a lang
Driving University Avenue, 19 and wild and free
O baby baby shoop shoop it's so beautiful you here with me

I've attended the State Fair almost every year
Since 1948 and watched the giant walleyes
Glide in their tank and sat on the John Deere,
Rode the double Ferris, ate the curly fries,
The corndogs, bumped through Ye Old Mill,
The boats in a dark tunnel in the cold water,
And it's so much the same that time stands still,
Especially when I come here with my daughter.
When I walk the Midway with her again
And smell the sawdust and hot dogs, I remember
How right, how delicious it was to be ten
In August, smelling the approach of September,
But now I am sixty-six and (good God) terrified,
Thinking of death at the top of the Giant Slide.

Bring me a pizza and a bottle of beer
You women come right in here
Turn that music up good and loud
This isn't church this is a dancing crowd
You intellectuals shut your traps
Get up and dance and shake your laps
Tonight let's all be loose and frec
Forget the University
The lonely journeys of the mind
Give me synchronicity
With those in front and those behind
Dance does more than philosophy
To raise us mortals toward the sky
So said Shakespeare so say I

My novel has sold well (thank you, Lord)
And made the big best-seller lists
So let's go home and lock the door
And practice being hedonists.
For years the old wolf lay in wait
Beside the door, about to pounce,
So we're prepared to appreciate
Caviar at $100 the ounce
And a Montalcino— an '82!
Outrageously expensive.
Nothing's too good for me and you
Tonight. What is the sense of
Self-denial? We did that for years.
Here's to joyful excess. Cheers.

How is your bookstore doing? people ask, and I say,
"Holding its own." And they smile and say, Great.
A bookstore is like an old father. If he has a nice day,
Goes for a walk: fine. It's enough to perambulate,
No need to run a six-minute mile.
A bookstore is for people who love books and need
To touch them, open them, browse for awhile,
And find some common good— that's why we read.
Readers and writers are two sides of the same gold coin.
You write and I read and in that moment I find
A union more perfect than any club I could join:
The simple intimacy of being one mind.
　　Here in a book-filled sun-lit room below the street,
　　Strangers— some living, some dead— are hoping to
meet.

A little girl is singing for the faithful to come ye
Joyful and triumphant, a song she loves,
And also the partridge in a pear tree
And the golden rings and the turtle doves.
In the dark streets, red lights and green and blue
Where the faithful live, some joyful, some troubled,
Enduring the cold and also the flu,
Taking the garbage out and keeping the sidewalk shoveled.
Not much triumph going on here— and yet
There is much we do not understand.
And my hopes and fears are met
In this small singer holding onto my hand.
 Onward we go, faithfully, into the dark
  And are there angels singing overhead? Hark.

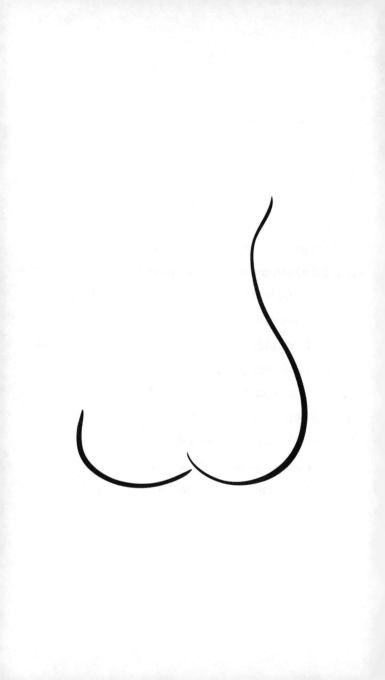

6

THE GODS OF CLEAN SHEETS

Hanging out on the frozen steppes of Minnesota
In February, the Mississippi, that mighty river,
A long glacier, I think back to that hotel
That night, my love, and wonder if life will ever
Be so good as when you, cell phone in hand,
Tall and possessed of extravagant nerve,
Guided me lost in town in the white Dodge van
To where you stood grinning on the curb.
Climbed in and said hi and through the palmy streets
To Joe's Cafe for gin and quesadillas—
And all that followed as the gods of clean sheets
Looked up and laughed and laughed to see us.
Our clothing scattered and the dancing slow,
Our lips, our hips, us slipping to and fro.

THE BEACH

This morning she awoke my dear lover
on the bed on her back buck naked
and I crept under the cotton sky and over
a hill with tufts of sea grass and snaked
myself into a ravine and there found
a delicate creature trembling with sensation
a pink anemone that I touched and (whoa) the sound
of a soprano singing Italian German and Croatian
simultaneously and so I put my tongue
to it and tasted caviar and Cabernet
and from above was softly sung
a Puccini aria by Billie Holiday
so prettily and then a shudder and a sigh
and we lay quietly the opera star and I

She reclining nude and pale and unconcerned
At being stared at and so I am glad to stare
At her long legs and arms and torso turned
Toward me, pink from the shower, her dark hair
Splayed wet on the pillow, the pale chapel
Of her ribcage and the curvature
Of her belly like Michelangelo's marble,
A face worthy of great literature.
Next week she leaves for China. Six weeks.
The mind is dumb with grief. Perhaps she'll find
Someone she likes better, a man who speaks
To some untouched corner of her mind,
And I will lose her— O my lost Lenore!
And now the great bird is tapping at the door.

A series of defeats has brought me to this
Dark room where, against the teachings of the church,
We lie in the tremendous dark and kiss
And loosen our clothing and yield to the urge
Of nakedness and sensibility,
The delicious unbuttoning, and you see me
Undefended. Naked. The civility
Of you on my skin, vast and dreamy
As Montana and now I am heading west
On a winding road through the dark contours
Of mountain latitudes, coming to rest
In a meadow of tender grasses of amour.
    This is what I drove across North Dakota to find:
    This tenderness. And put all my failed life behind.

Being in love means sailing at a fever pitch,
Engines pounding, men in the boiler room
Shoveling coal, the ship racing to port, which
Is apt to switch suddenly— she's in Khartoum
Now, not Rangoon— Khartoum— so we go
There, sleet in our faces, the wind rises
And the heart soars or the heart sinks low
And it's just endless— like the Mideast crisis—
But what can I do? Darling, you seduced me
Completely. Just as I was ready to hang
Up my sextant and get off the sea
And take up farming, the telephone rang.
    And here I go— off to the Hebrides or the Azores.
    Because you said those things and now I'm yours.

THE INTERSECTION

A man will go to great lengths to find affection,
risking shame & disgrace— I think of those
I saw once at a Minneapolis intersection
Cruising among other men in ice & snow,
Angling, parading, hoping to find the one
With whom they would not feel so alone
& hold him close & do whatever is done
Physically— & all simply to be KNOWN
By another— O it is a moving sight,
How much we need another & I need you,
My darling you a world away tonight,
So I write this poem. What else to do?
I know by heart your hands & face & lips & hair
And hold you close to me though you are way out there.

ENGULFED

I am engulfed by you and almost drowned
For love of you— one look at your face meant
Bridges down, streets flooded for miles around,
Three feet of water in the basement,
And a tall blonde newswoman on my lawn
Saying, "The man is in love— no end in sight.
The forecast is for this romance to go on and on."
I watch her on TV and I can see she's right.
I pack my bags. I would like to apologize
For my heart that has caused so much damage,
The tides of passion that bust up old ties
As casually as a man chews a tuna sandwich.
I walk away from the ruins and get in my car,
Drive out of town and wonder where you are.

I wake up in the morning, eat some cantaloupe,
Toast two slices of bread, pour hot water through
The coffee, read about Obama and the pope
And think tenderly of faraway you.
A cold day in hell and my soul is haunted.
I am a ghost here. All I ever wanted,
My love, is to be in your arms, my love.
You're flying to the rainy plains of Spain
And I'm snowbound alone on a rather grand
Street in St. Paul going quietly insane,
Wishing you'd call or something. I stand
At the window as if you might suddenly appear.
O I would give anything— anything! Do you hear
Me, love?— if I could be in your arms, my love.

A man ought to guard his heart, not spend
His salary on the cloths of heaven and lavish
Love as I have on you, my darling friend,
And now, calling you out of fear and anguish
And loneliness, I detect in your voice a slight
Tone of indifference there in the hotel
In Barcelona where you're seeing the sights,
And it rips my heart— how your voice fell
When you heard mine, your old lover—
O darling I am suddenly 14 years old and dying,
Holding the phone, trembling to discover
That Karen has gone to the dance with Brian.

    Guarding the heart. Too late. Mine is gone,
    Left in San Francisco, like in the song.

Your therapist said we should break up so we did.
I'm all wrong for you and unavailable and too old
And so for your sake, I've cut you loose, kid,
And gone back to the land of snow and cold.
I try not to think about you but I do, every minute,
And now the crocuses have bloomed
And every blossom has your name spelled in it
And everywhere romance is resumed—
Just as I thrived in your arms a month ago,
Leaning toward the gleam in your green eye,
Walking through the parking lot, row on row,
To the terminal and saying a long sad goodbye.
    I did it for you and wish I knew what I've done,
    Walking away from you that day, my darling one.

Why have I spent so much in a hopeless cause,
This year of love that plainly goes nowhere
But to a disheveled day of unspeakable loss
Which has arrived: your letter, my dear,
Saying that you love me but you're moving on,
Which you should do. I know it. But O love of mine—
I walked the street last night, weeping. Dawn
Came up on my second cup of coffee. Sunshine
Pours down on these eyes in their damp caves.
The loss of you destroys me, I who have stood
Calmly amid weeping and looked down into the graves
Of loved ones — nothing will ever be so good

 Again as lying, heart thumping, beside you in bed.
 And now my heart is forced to listen to my head.

DEEP HOLE

Now that you're gone, I see that what I miss
Most is the dreamy look of sweet surprise
On your upturned face and the coffee kiss
And your tongue and your soft animal sighs,
My hands on your hips, your lips nibbling at mine—
How well our bodies merged in a close space,
Our noses side by side, your hair like dark vines
Framing the portrait of your opulent face.
O the tides of time are cruel, my love, so cruel
And what is lost is not to be regained, I fear,
And so I am cast down into a deep hole,
Standing and watching you slowly disappear.
Have mercy on this grievous sinner, O Lord.
She is gone gone gone who was my joy and more.

TO HER NEXT LOVER

She's a good woman, keep that in mind
As you are engaged with her other features,
Her delicious breasts, her long legs that she will wind
Around your waist— O she is a marvel, this creature,
When she lies back, her eyes shut, and her
Pleasure is the song of long-tailed coastal birds.
I hope you give her great pleasure, sir,
Though I do choke a little on those words.
If you hit her, you will go straight to hell.
If you cheat on her, you are a fool. So
Be as good to her as you know how. I wish you well
Though cast down in grief to see her go.

    She and I were happy together for so long
    And I love her no less now that she is gone.

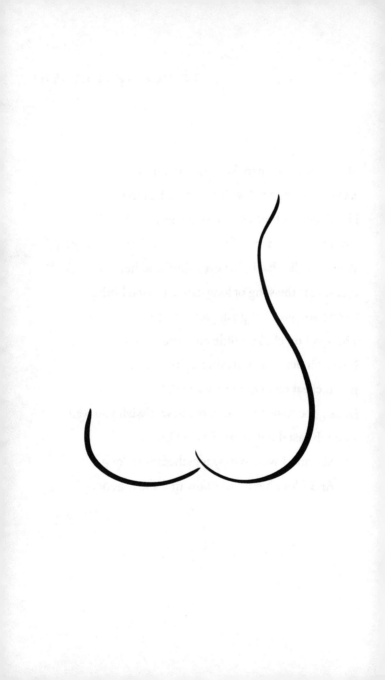

7

SONNET FOR A MAJOR BIRTHDAY

It was a birthday I had dreaded for months,
The creaking door to Ancient & Historic,
And I thought how I was so lively once
And never would be again (alas, poor Yorick),
And then the day itself, so very ordinary,
Quiet, partly cloudy, warm. Swift.
One more August day on our extensive prairie,
And ordinariness was my birthday gift.
Nothing happened. Coffee, fried eggs, and bacon,
A hot shower, the ordinary stuff of happiness,
To which I hope every morning to awaken
Until one day I don't, which is not for me to guess.
Thirty, forty, fifty, and then (O my God) sixty-five,
But it's okay— you wake up, you yawn, you're still alive.

O radio listeners, I think of you with gratitude,
Tuned in, simmering tomato sauce, trying not to boil it,
Or biking with headphones, or reclining nude
In the bathtub, the radio perched on the toilet.
Every week I think about you listening to my show,
Though I realize that listening is erratic,
And that many of you turn the volume very low
So as to make my voice a sort of murmury static,
Like the whisper of leaves in a poplar tree.
But two weeks ago, a girl with green eyes
Told me that the show is cool, and this to me
Was worth more than a Pulitzer Prize.
She was sixteen and pretty cool herself. It made me glad,
A real compliment from a friend I didn't know I had.

I lie down at night with this cold dumb dread
Of death's dark estate, and that is why
I don't mind you kicking me in bed.
Not at all. I'd rather be kicked than die.
It must be so boring to lie down dead
After the long gloopy memorial goodbye
And contemplate what you wish you'd said
For your Last Words— No, I prefer to lie
Spooned with you until I'm ninety or ninety-five,
Still crazy about you, and say goodnight one night
And dream I am saved by grace and then dive
Swanlike into a spacious tunnel of celestial light.

    Out with the old and in with the shining new,
    Hello Jesus, goodbye O marvelous you.

They say life is short but actually it's as long as it is.
A day with two lawyers can last for months,
Whereas my forty-third year went by in a whiz.
And the marriage to Lulu vanished all at once.

So what If I knew I had one day to live?
I'd spend it looking deep into your eyes,
Watching you breathe, hearing your musical sighs
As life dripped away like wine through a silver sieve.

Morning, noon, and night, all my final day,
I would gaze at you, love, and not look away.
Your hair streaked with blonde, your elegant nose,
The liquid liquefaction of your clothes.
One last waltz and then God shows me the door.
Perfectly okay. I couldn't ask for more.

Let's find a place on Park Avenue
And a pied-a-terre in Paris, France,
And I will sit and worship you
In yellow rooms with potted plants.
Me, a somewhat endearing relic,
A crinkly old literary man,
And you, tall, dark, angelic
Reclining prettily on a silk divan.

And if you leave me after awhile,
I'll go live at the Hotel Carlyle
With Egyptian sheets and fresh-cut flowers
And room service 24 hours.
They'll bring me champagne and caviar
And when I die, they'll send a car.

My love is like a red red rose but also like daffodils
Who haste away too soon for time is flying
And this splendor in the grass, like birds' madrigals,
Is fading in the west. Egypt, we are dying.
You lived with me and were my love and we proved
All the pleasures and gathered rosebuds while we could
And now we're old and the kids have moved
Us to the Christopher Marlowe Care Center where good
Christian women serve us a daffodil consommé
And there are madrigals every Tuesday, my love,
My love, and in physical therapy class we play
A small guitar and sing to the stars above,

    "What a beautiful pussy!" and a five-pound note
    Flutters from the heavens and that is all she wrote.

Here we sit as evening falls
Like old horses in their stalls.
Thank you, Father, that you bless
Us with food and an address
And the comfort of your hand
In this great and blessed land.
Look around at each dear face,
Keep each one in your good grace.
We think of those who went before,
And wish we could have loved them more.
Grant to us a cheerful heart,
Knowing we must soon depart
To that far land to be with them.
And now let's eat. Praise God. Amen.